LIVING on the VEG

BY CLIVE GIFFORD
RECIPES BY JACQUELINE MELDR

Published in paperback in Great Britain in 2020 by Wayland
Text copyright © Hodder and Stoughton, 2018

Editor: Sarah Peutrill
Designer: Lisa Peacock
Cover illustrations: Sara Mulvanny
Cover design: Rawshock Design

Picture credits:
Illustrations © Sara Mulvanny: Cover, 8–9, 13, 20, 24–25, 31, 35, 42b, 43b, 44–45, 48, 50, 51l, 53b.
Photos: 4: Jane McAdam. 5: Sarah Trivuncic. 15: imging/Shutterstock. 34t: Fascinadora/Shutterstock. 34b: Joe Gough/Shutterstock. 36: Bartosz Luczak/Shutterstock. 49: stockcreations/Shutterstock. 51: Matushchak Anton/Shutterstock.
Recipe photos (pp52–75) © Jacqueline Meldrum.
All other illustration and design elements: Shutterstock.
Every attempt has been made to clear copyright. Should there be any inadvertent omission please apply to the publisher for rectification.

ISBN: 978 1 5263 0610 4

The website addresses (URLs) included in this book were valid at the time of going to press. However, it is possible that contents or addresses may have changed since the publication of this book. No responsibility for any such changes can be accepted by either the author or the Publisher.

FSC
www.fsc.org

MIX
Paper from responsible sources
FSC® C104740

www.hachette.co.uk

www.hachettechildrens.co.uk

The recipes in this book are designed to be made by children. However, we recommend adult supervision at all times. The Publishers and the authors cannot accept any legal responsibility or liability for accidents or damage arising from making the recipes. Some of the recipes may involve nuts or seeds. Anyone with a known nut allergy must avoid these.

CONTENTS

FOREWORD

CLIVE

I've been vegetarian for over 25 years. It started when I backpacked around the world and encountered a wide range of amazing cultures, foods and ways of living and treating animals. I returned home eager to know more about how the food I ate was produced. I was shocked by what I learned.

I knew I couldn't save the world all by myself but wanted to make my own contribution, mostly to reduce animal cruelty and my impact on the planet. So, I began living on the veg and have never looked back.

IT'S NOT ALL BEEN PLAIN SAILING, especially at first with teasing from friends, cookery chaos and restaurant roulette. Even today, living a vegetarian lifestyle does require more thought than just going with the meat-eating flow. But with veggie food so varied, tasty and downright fun, I think the effort is well worth it and I hope you find the book interesting and useful.

JACQUELINE

Like Clive, I've been vegetarian for over 25 years. I made the change to a full vegetarian diet when I left home to go to art college. Back then there wasn't a lot of choice for vegetarians in supermarkets, so you had to be quite creative if you wanted to have a varied and interesting diet.

Unfortunately, I could only cook a few meals and for years most of those meals started with a tin of tomatoes. I was boring myself and boring my veggie husband, so I started a food blog to encourage myself to try new dishes. I called my blog Tinned Tomatoes as a reminder to be adventurous.

MY BLOG has thousands of visitors every day from all over the world looking for new recipes and following the adventures of my veggie family. I wish you luck on your veggie journey and hope you enjoy the recipes in this book.

GOING VEGGIE

If you're thinking of turning vegetarian and living on the veg or have already taken the first step, remember this:

YOU ARE NOT ALONE!

There are thought to be some 375 MILLION full-time veggies worldwide. Millions more enjoy meat-free meals regularly but still eat some meat or fish. Most veggies enjoy their mealtimes just as much as meat-eaters, as they rustle up and chow down on inventive, varied and mouth-watering meals or grab scrummy snacks to go.

Vegetarianism has a long, long history in civilisations stretching back to ancient Egypt (see pages 8–9). But in the past 25 years, turning veggie has become a whole lot easier with new meat-free products, a wider, more varied range of foods available in stores and restaurants and the rise of the Internet and social media allowing veggies to share recipes, advice, places to go and words of support.

This book will guide you through some of the key reasons why people turn vegetarian, from reducing ANIMAL CRUELTY TO HEALTH, RELIGIOUS BELIEFS AND PROTECTING THE ENVIRONMENT. It will explain the difference between vegetarians, vegans and pescetarians and the sorts of questions new vegetarians are often asked. It will also provide you with plenty to think about as well as lots of tips for living a veggie life including making your own veggie snacks and meals, breaking the news to others and building a meat-free diet that is just as healthy as it is tasty.

"Every time we sit down to eat, we make a choice: please choose vegetarianism. Do it for animals. Do it for the environment and do it for your health."
– ALEC BALDWIN, ACTOR

YE OLDE VEGETARIAN

Vegetarianism may seem fashionable and trendy today, but it actually has a long history. People living in the Indus Valley, ancient Greece and India, for example, followed their own form of vegetarianism more than 2,500 years ago.

According to the Vegetarian Society, some ancient Egyptians more than 5,000 years ago refrained from eating meat or wearing clothing made of animal products. Ancient Greek philosopher, Pythagoras and his followers believed that all living creatures had souls and thus it was wrong to kill them for food.

In Europe, the first organisation to abandon meat eating was the Bible Christian Church in the early 1800s in Manchester, England. Martha Brotherton, a member of the church, published a pioneering book *Vegetable Cookery* in 1833. Fourteen years later, the Vegetarian Society was formed, also in Manchester, followed by the American Vegetarian Society in 1850.

SOME FAMOUS VEGETARIANS FROM HISTORY

EMPEROR TENMU OF JAPAN
REIGNED 673–686

LEONARDO DA VINCI, INVENTOR AND ARTIST
1452–1519

MARY SHELLEY, AUTHOR
1797–1851

LOUISA MAY ALCOTT, AUTHOR
1832–1888

MOHANDAS GHANDI, CAMPAIGNER
1869–1948

ROSA PARKS, ACTIVIST
1913–2005

British poet PERCY SHELLEY turned vegetarian in 1812 and was amongst the first to point out how the meat industry used up and wasted natural resources which could be put to better use. His wife MARY SHELLEY, the author of *Frankenstein*, was also vegetarian.

This viewpoint was reinforced by a number of writers in the 1960s and 1970s onwards, particularly FRANCES MOORE LAPPÉ. In 1971, she wrote the best-selling book, *Diet For A Small Planet*, in which she argued that a meat-free diet was essential to feeding the world because plant-based foods have less impact on the environment than meat. This book and others sparked a major interest in vegetarianism which continues to this day.

WHAT'S IN A NAME?

Whilst people have followed vegetarian diets for thousands of years, the word itself was not used until the 19th century. Vegetarians avoid eating meat, fish and shellfish and foods made from animal parts such as gelatine (see page 38). As a simple guide, if a creature had to die in order to produce what you are eating, then that food is not vegetarian-friendly.

OVO-LACTO VEGETARIAN

This is most vegetarians. They eat eggs (the 'ovo' part) and dairy products (the 'lacto' part), such as milk and cheese. Some vegetarians choose to avoid eggs (which are never fertilised so do not contain infant chicks) for health (see page 30) or humane reasons, due to how battery hens are kept (see page 15).

PESCETARIAN

These are people who do not eat meat or poultry (chicken, duck, turkey) but do eat fish and/or shellfish such as prawns, crabs or scallops. Some refer to themselves still as vegetarian ... but they're not!

FLEXITARIAN

This modern term is sometimes used for people who reduce their meat and fish consumption greatly but still eat it on occasion. Flexitarians argue that they are still making a contribution by cutting down their meat consumption and many avoid factory-farmed meat products, choosing to eat free-range or organic meat.

VEGAN

Vegans do not eat any animal products whatsoever. This not only includes meat, fish and shellfish but also eggs and dairy products. It also includes foodstuffs produced by creatures such as bees and animal materials and products such as leather, wool and silk. A vegan diet can give you all the essential nutrients you need, but vegans do have to be careful to ensure they eat a wide variety of foods to obtain all the nutrients their bodies need.

WHY TURN VEGGIE?

THERE ARE MANY DIFFERENT REASONS PEOPLE TURN VEGGIE.

For some, it is simply the taste or texture of meat and fish they do not like or the view that a diet free of meat is healthier (see page 30). For others, it might be a mixture of reasons involving their personal beliefs, concerns about animal welfare or how not eating meat can help the planet and people on it.

NO MEAT BELIEFS

A number of religions hold that as
their god or gods created all animal life, it is wrong for
people to take life unnecessarily when other foods exist.
The principle of *ahisma* – non-injuring or avoiding doing
harm – is part of a number of Asian religions including
Buddhism, Hinduism and Jainism. All followers of Jainism
are vegetarians, as are a number of Buddhists and around
30 per cent of Hindus. Some groups within other
religions, like the Taoists, choose to be vegetarian.

ANIMAL WELFARE

Some people turn veggie because they just cannot face eating animals. Others are horrified by the way animals are reared for slaughter and want to do their bit to reduce animal cruelty.

Despite a rise in free-range farming, where creatures are given space to roam outdoors, most meat is factory farmed in large-scale operations. Animal young are separated quickly from their mothers and are sometimes fed antibiotics and other drugs to grow faster than they would naturally, putting such a strain on their bodies that some cannot walk.

Frequently, the creatures are so crammed into sheds that they cannot turn around or lie down. FACTORY-FARMED CHICKENS, for instance, live their entire lives inside huge sheds, with no access to the outdoors. Machines automatically fill up food and water feeders. The chickens breathe in the strong smell of their own poo all day and night. As they grow bigger, space to move around becomes tighter and tighter. Many animals suffer disease and stress living in cramped, filthy and unnatural conditions.

Come slaughter time, animals are often shipped long distances packed tightly into containers. Despite laws in some countries insisting on creatures being unconscious before they are killed, many are not slaughtered humanely, but are left stunned and in pain, to bleed or suffocate to death.

PLANET IN PERIL

Four times more meat is consumed today than 50 years ago. More THAN 56 THOUSAND MILLION FARM ANIMALS are now killed each year to produce 308 MILLION TONNES OF MEAT. This giant industry has a massive impact on Earth, much of it negative. Many turn veggie, believing that less meat-eating will equal less impact.

GRAZING

Today, according to the United Nations (UN), more than a quarter of all the ice-free land on Earth – not just farmland – is used for farm animals to graze on. Much of this land was once bushland, plains or forest offering habitats to a wide range of different plant and animal species. As more land is cleared for grazing, so the number of different species of living things it can support drops sharply, endangering plant and animal life.

REARING MEAT IS A REAL LAND HOG!

WATER WASTE

Seven-tenths of all the fresh water taken from rivers, streams, lakes and underground sources is used in farming. Rearing meat requires vast quantities, both for animals to drink and to water the crops and plants they consume. With shortages of clean water already affecting hundreds of millions of people across the planet, can we afford to continue to use so much water in meat production?

DEFORESTATION AND SOIL EROSION

Clearing land of trees loses habitats and increases greenhouse gas emissions (see page 19). Between 1970 and 2016, deforestation saw Brazil lose over 768,000 km^2 of Amazon rainforest – an area more than twice the size of Germany. About 70 per cent of this forest was cleared to create grazing land for farm animals. Grazing animals cause further damage, stripping land of plants whose roots bind the soil together. Soil erosion can turn fertile land into desert or semi-desert, unable to support as much life as before.

WATER REQUIRED TO GROW 1 KG OF FOOD

287 litres   2,500 litres   15,400 litres

POLLUTING THE PLANET

The meat industry also affects water (and land) in another way — POLLUTION. Animals raised for food produce more than 120 TIMES the amount of POO than the entire world human population. This, and potentially harmful chemicals such as fertilisers, seep into the land or run-off into nearby streams and rivers. There, they can build up, killing creatures and damaging life in the water.

OUT AT SEA

Over 150 million tonnes of fish are caught in the world's seas and oceans each year. A tragic consequence of all this fishing is the death of 300,000 dolphins, whales and porpoises accidentally caught in nets or fishing tackle. Over-fishing of some species and parts of the sea has devastated life in the water and threatened some creatures with extinction. When one creature dwindles or dies out, it can damage food chains meaning other sea creatures are threatened.

Why Turn Veggie?

MEAT AND CLIMATE CHANGE

Climate change is a big issue and meat plays a surprisingly big part. You probably know that GREENHOUSE GASES, such as carbon dioxide (CO_2), in the atmosphere help warm the planet by trapping heat. In recent times, increases in greenhouse gases caused by human activity have caused more heat to be trapped, leading to global warming. What you might not know is that according to UN report, *Livestock's Long Shadow*, at least 18 per cent of all greenhouse gases are produced by livestock. This means that FARMED ANIMALS PRODUCE MORE GREENHOUSE GASES THAN ALL THE WORLD'S CARS, BUSES, PLANES, SHIPS AND TRAINS PUT TOGETHER.

CARBON DIOXIDE

CO_2 travels into the atmosphere when fossil fuels are burned but also when forests are cleared for grazing and for growing crops, much of which is devoted to producing food for animals.

METHANE

Each one of the 1.4 billion cows on the planet can produce 500 litres of methane gas each day through flatulence and manure. Methane has 25 times more impact on global warming than CO_2.

NITROUS OXIDE

Almost two-thirds of nitrous oxide produced by human activity is from farming animals and the vast amounts of manure they produce.

A WASTEFUL WORLD

People have got to eat, and even vegetarians and vegans have a negative impact on the planet through crop farming. However, some people turn vegetarian because they believe choosing plants over meat is less wasteful. Only a small fraction of the energy in plants is turned into meat which can be eaten. The rest is used by the creature to grow, move and keep warm.

According to the Vegetarian and Vegan Foundation, as much as 17 kg of protein from plants is needed to produce just 1 kg of meat protein. Some ask, why couldn't the plant protein go directly to human mouths and generate vastly more food and with less impact on the planet?

SOLVING WORLD HUNGER

According to *The American Journal of Clinical Nutrition*, a meat-eater's diet requires **17 TIMES MORE LAND, 14 TIMES MORE WATER AND 10 TIMES MORE ENERGY** than a vegetarian's. Many turn veggie in the hope that their less wasteful diet would enable more of the planet's people to gain the food they need.

Hunger, though, is a complex issue because of the way food and wealth is distributed around the world and the gap between wealthy, developed nations who tend to eat far more meat than the inhabitants of poorer, developing countries. A study in 2009, for example, found that each American eats an average of **120 KG** of meat per year, **30 TIMES** the amount of the average Bangladeshi.

What is not in question is that lack of food is a very real threat to many, with some **795 MILLION PEOPLE FACING HUNGER** in 2016. This is not missing out on the odd meal, but a painful and desperate desire for food due to not having eaten enough nutrients to sustain your body. Around **21,000 PEOPLE DIE** each day from starvation or hunger-related diseases. UNICEF estimate that a further **161 MILLION UNDER-5s** – twice the entire population of Germany – suffer from stunted growth as a result of hunger.

HELP ME FEED MYSELF.

QUESTIONS, QUESTIONS

If you turn veggie, one thing you can certainly expect is a whole raft of questions as you're quizzed by friends, family and sometimes even complete strangers! In this chapter are some of the most commonly-asked question or debate points along with answers you might find helpful.

"How can he practice true compassion who eats the flesh of an animal to fatten his own flesh?" –

THIRUVALLUVAR, TAMIL POET AND PHILOSOPHER

Q: DON'T YOU HAVE TO EAT MEAT TO BE STRONG?

A: Ask a rhino or an elephant! These creatures eat plants and no one's calling them a weakling! Nor would you label nine-time Olympic gold medal winning vegetarian runner, Paavo Nurmi, puny. Others include Olympic cycling champion, Lizzie Armistead, vegetarian since the age of 10, and Olympic gold medal winning runner Carl Lewis, who turned vegetarian after he'd won one set of medals and went on to win more, fuelled by his plant-based diet. Like all athletes, these sportspeople are very serious about what they eat and receive a lot of advice from nutrition experts. Meat can, of course, provide lots of protein and nutrients such as iron and vitamin B12, but as pages 32–33 show, there are lots of non-meat sources beside.

Q. ISN'T VEGGIE FOOD DIFFICULT AND TIME-CONSUMING TO COOK?

A. How difficult is a jacket spud topped with baked beans or a bowl of pasta in a simple tomato sauce? And how long does it take to warm pitta pockets and serve it with hummus and grilled mushrooms and courgettes? Many veggie meals are quick and easy to make. Some can be eaten cold or frozen for a later date meaning one cooking session can produce two or three meals.

Q. Isn't veggie food bland and samey?

After a plate of tasteless value meat sausages, you could say the same about meaty meals! Like all meals, veggie dishes can be bland or tasty, depending on the ingredients and the way they are prepared and cooked. Neither does going veggie mean endless salads. There are thousands of veggie recipes online helping to create varied meals, from tofu 'fish' fingers and wild mushroom ravioli, to smoked tofu goulash or creamy coconut curry.

Q. IF EVERYONE TURNED VEGETARIAN TOMORROW, WOULDN'T WE BE OVERRUN WITH ANIMALS?

A. Yes, at first, if such an unlikely event were to occur! After all, a global count made in 2014 revealed there were around 1.4 billion cattle, 986 million pigs and 21.3 billion chickens on the planet. But, what is more likely is gradual rather than overnight change, with demand for meat dropping slowly over time. This would mean fewer animals being bred for meat and numbers dropping naturally. Those remaining could be left to live on some of the large areas of land previously devoted to livestock farming.

Q. IF EVERYONE ELSE KEEPS EATING MEAT, WHAT'S THE POINT?

A. The majority of the world does eat meat, but the number of vegetarians is growing. All these people are making a difference. Together, they have already helped propel restaurants and supermarkets into stocking vegetarian meals and influenced others into reducing how much meat they eat. In the United States, for example, the amount of red meat each person consumes has dropped by almost 15 per cent between 2005 and 2015. Individually, each new vegetarian makes their own important contribution, especially when you consider that a typical meat-eater in the US or UK consumes over 7,000 creatures during their lifetime.

Q. Isn't eating meat natural for people?

This question causes much debate. Some people point to the four pointed canine teeth in our mouths as proof of people being natural meat-eaters. These are the sorts of teeth found in carnivorous (meat-eating) creatures. Others, though, point out that our canines are puny compared to real carnivores, like tigers, plus we have teeth they lack – long rows of molars and pre-molars designed to grind up plant matter. Our 7-m-long digestive system has much in common with plant-eating creatures but we can digest meat too. Being able to digest plants and meat saved humans from starvation thousands of years ago when people didn't have the same food choices as we do today.

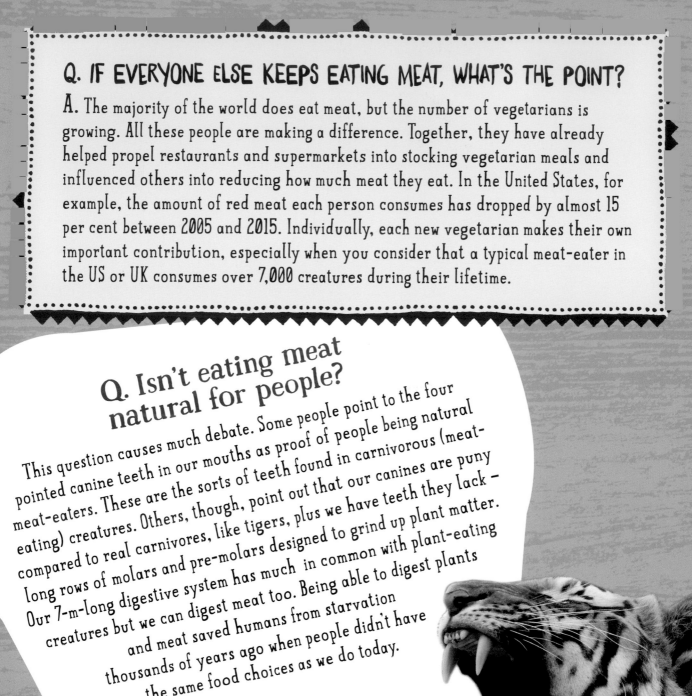

Q. IF MANY DIFFERENT ANIMALS ALL KILL FOR FOOD, WHY SHOULDN'T WE?

A. Creatures do a lot of things we don't, couldn't or shouldn't do – from some female spiders eating male spiders after mating to dogs sniffing each other's bottoms! Carnivores, such as lions and tigers, are animals who rely on eating meat to survive. Humans are actually omnivorous; they are capable of eating both meat and plants to survive. So, as an omnivore, you have the choice to eat meat or not.

Q. BUT DOESN'T FRUIT AND VEG FEEL PAIN AND PLANTS SCREAM WHEN PULLED OUT OF THE GROUND?

A. This is a myth that makes many vegetarians scream, not plants! Scientists have detected faint sounds when plants are cut or pulled out of the ground. These, though, are simply gas leaving the plant and not a scream of agony. Plants have no nervous system or sensors so cannot feel pain. And even if plants did feel pain, meat-eaters are actually responsible for far more plants being consumed than veggies due to the large amounts of plants animals raised for meat have to eat.

HEALTHY LIVING

Vegetarians can easily enjoy a healthy, happy diet, but only if they eat a balanced and varied range of foods. After all, chips, chocolate and cheese can all be vegetarian, but living solely off these items will lead to a growing gut and a lot of other health problems!

Don't forget to check out the recipe section from page 52 for some fantastic meal and snack ideas.

"After all the information I gathered about the mistreatment of animals, I couldn't continue to eat meat. The more I was aware of, the harder and harder it was to do ... There are no negatives to eating like this [vegan]. I feel nothing but positive, mentally and physically. I love it." -

- LIAM HEMSWORTH, HUNGER GAMES ACTOR

HEALTHY HEART AND BODY

A good veggie diet can potentially be a lot healthier than one based heavily on meat which tends to contain a lot of SATURATED FATS. Even lean minced beef has more than four times the fat of beans and chickpeas. In addition, large numbers of veggies eat a lot more FIBRE in their diet than meat-eaters. Many scientific studies have shown that a diet heavy in saturated fats can increase the chances of suffering from heart disease. Vegetarians who eat well may also be less at risk of high blood pressure, strokes and diabetes.

HEARD IT ALL BEFORE?

You've probably learned a lot about diet at school. All the key points made in those lessons – from eating plenty of fruit and veg to not over-indulging in sugary or fatty foods – still apply to you. Turning veggie does not make you super-healthy overnight or able to skip nutrition lessons. If anything, you need to be more aware of what nutrients you need so that you can ensure you get them and in the right quantities.

FOOD GROUPS

Different countries use different ways of getting across what a healthy diet consists of like this food plate. Everyone, whether veggie or not, needs a balanced and varied diet containing: protein, carbohydrate, fat, sugar, vitamins and minerals in the right proportions.

FRUIT AND VEG

CARBOHYDRATES

PULSES

SUGAR

DAIRY

This plate gives a guide to the right amounts of different food types you should tuck into each day.

FINDING REPLACEMENTS

Meat and fish provide your body with protein and certain essential vitamins and minerals. So, it's important that you gain these nutrients – particularly vitamins D and B12 and the mineral, iron – from alternative, meat-free, sources*.

DELVE INTO B12

VITAMIN B12 is needed for your body to grow and repair itself. It is only found in animal products but that includes milk, cheese and eggs so if you're an ovo-lacto veggie (see page 10), you should be fine. Alternative sources are cereals to which B12 has been added (known as 'fortified' and shown on the ingredients label) and fortified yeast extract such as Marmite.

VITAMIN D

This vitamin is thought to help with the health of your bones, muscles and immune and nervous systems. Eggs contain it as does milk fortified with VITAMIN D. If you are vegan or don't drink dairy milk, then it is often found in fortified soya and almond milk and yoghurt alternatives.

* Vegans may find they need to take vitamin and iron supplements as well. See page 76 for more on this.

IRON IN

Small amounts of **iRON** help keep your blood healthy and enable it to transport oxygen around your body for respiration – the chemical process which releases energy from food. Iron is found in red meat but also lots of other sources including eggs, tofu, green vegetables such as spinach and pak choi, soya, kidney beans, dried apricots, raisins, figs, lentils and chickpeas.

»→ POINTS ABOUT PROTEIN ←«

PROTEIN is a crucial food group. It consists of building block substances called amino acids which help you develop and grow, and your body to repair itself. Meats and fish tend to contain all or almost all the amino acids whilst proteins found in plants often contain just some. So, you need to eat a wide and varied range of different protein-rich veggie foods to get the lot.

Fortunately, there are a vast range of sources of protein suitable for veggies. These are sometimes split into the four broad groups shown here, with some examples:

NUTS AND SEEDS:
brazil nuts, almonds, quinoa, sunflower seeds, pumpkin seeds

EGGS AND DAIRY:
eggs, cheese, milk, yoghurt

GRAINS AND CEREALS:
oats, wheat, rice, bran

PULSES:
all types of beans including kidney, fava, soya and baked beans, peas, lentils, chickpeas

DON'T GO NUTS!

Don't go nuts about nuts – just a small number will help top up your protein levels as nuts are high in protein, but also high in fat. Some flaked almonds sprinkled over many dishes make a tasty, textured topping whilst a small handful of pecans or walnuts can be added to many hot veggie dishes or a few cashews can be mixed into a stir-fry.

CARB LOADING

Starchy foods like bread, potatoes, pasta, rice and cereal contain lots of carbohydrates. These are essential for activity as they are quick, reliable sources of energy which your body can convert rapidly. The vegetarian society advises children to eat FIVE PORTIONS OF STARCHY FOOD A DAY – not a problem for veggies intent on enjoying meals involving pasta, rice and grains such as couscous. How you eat these foods, though, is crucial. Five portions of chips fried in oil or white toast dripping in butter or high fat spread isn't going to do you as much good as a baked potato, some wholemeal bread and a portion of brown rice or wholegrain cereal.

FATS AND SUGAR

Typical isn't it? The things that many people most enjoy — from chocolate bars to fizzy drinks and fried foods — seem to be ram-packed with fat, sugar or both. Here are **FIVE TIPS** to help keep your **FAT AND SUGAR** levels under control:

- Drink water or sometimes milk. If you really miss fizzy drinks, try a little fruit juice or low-calorie squash diluted with lots of still or sparkling water.

- Try a sliced banana or avocado on toast instead of honey or butter.

- Switch your sweet snack from chocolate, biscuits or sweets to fresh fruit and the occasional oatcake or plain currant bun.

- Choose grilled, baked or steamed foods over fried when you can.

- Try switching a few high-sugar or high-fat foods out of your diet, such as replacing sugary breakfast cereal with wholewheat cereal biscuits or granary bread toast. Instead of potato chips and crisps, give carrot or cucumber dipped in hummus a go.

EXOTIC INGREDIENTS

Say hello to some less well-known ingredients that can really help you on your veggie journey.

QUORN

This relative of mushrooms is high in protein and fibre, low in fat and versatile. Quorn mince, for example, has only 22 per cent of the fat found in lean beef mince. It exists in many forms from chunks for stir-frying to breadcrumbed nuggets and veggie hot dogs. Most Quorn products do contain some egg white so are not suitable for vegans although some vegan Quorn foods are available.

QUORN 'CHICKEN'

TEMPEH AND TOFU

Tempeh and tofu are two soya products. Others include milks, spreads and ready meals. Tofu is soya bean curd which is high in protein and low in fat. Tempeh is similar to tofu, made from soya, but usually firmer and more nutty-tasting. It can be sliced and cooked in a variety of ways such as small strips in a stir-fry or thin slices grilled with veggies in a delicious hot sandwich.

TVP

Another soya product, textured vegetable protein (TVP), often comes in dried (add water or sauce) or ready-to-use mince or chunks and can be used to mimic meat well in some minced dishes such as veggie lasagne or cannelloni. Some people shy away from TVP (and Quorn) for precisely this reason – it reminds them too much of meat.

AGAR-AGAR

Made from seaweed, this is a veggie-friendly alternative to gelatine (which is an animal product – see page 38). Agar-agar can be used to make delicious desserts such as jellies and cheesecakes.

IS IT ANIMAL FREE?

A surprising number of foods you might think of as veggie-friendly do contain meat or fish products. Most brands of Worcester sauce, for instance, contain anchovies (tiny fish). There are other surprises in store for those new to the veggie caper. The good news is that some organisations and food producers and sellers print symbols on products to help you out. Find out what this is where you live.

Hidden Surprises

Some animal products hide behind bland-sounding names or are listed as E-numbers on ingredients' labels.

Lanolin and stearic acid, for instance, are found in some chewing gums and are most frequently derived from animal fats. Gelatine (also known as E441) is found in some sweets, jellies and other desserts, but is actually made from skin, tendons and bones of animals boiled down to form a gel.

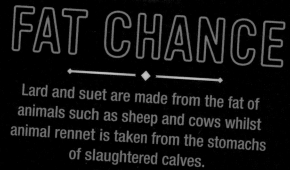

FAT CHANCE

Lard and suet are made from the fat of animals such as sheep and cows whilst animal rennet is taken from the stomachs of slaughtered calves.

It's found in cheeses such as grand-padano, parmesan and gorgonzola. If you're a cheese freak …relax. Lots of cheeses are made without rennet, but do check packaging just in case. And supermarkets stock vegetable suet, so you can still enjoy a steamed pudding.

INSECT INGREDIENTS

One key E-number to avoid is E120 (also known as carmine). It's used as a red dye in some yoghurts, ice creams and lipsticks and is made from the crushed bodies of Cochineal insects. It takes around 150,000 insects to make a single kilogram of colouring.

NOT JUST FOODS

Many veggies choose to avoid wearing animal products such as leather and silk which involve the death of creatures, but a surprising number of other things contain animal products. These include keratin (derived from animal hair, horns and hooves) in shampoos to scales of herring fish found in many shiny nail varnishes. There is also the issue of thousands of household products – from shampoos to cosmetics – which are tested on animals. This testing causes many thousands of animals to suffer and die every year. Organisations like PETA and Cruelty Free International keep long, searchable lists online of which products are not tested on animals. See page 76 for some useful websites.

A Veggie Life

SO YOU'VE THOUGHT LONG AND HARD ABOUT IT AND DECIDED TO LIVE LIFE ON THE VEG...

and fruit and lots of other tasty foods besides. What happens next? The most important thing to remember is that you shouldn't feel rushed or under pressure. If it's all too much in one go, you can take your time and gradually make changes as you work towards a goal of going meat-free. Some people, for example, begin by cutting out red meat or go veggie for a few days a week at first.

» → BRACE YOURSELF ← «

TAKING THE PLUNGE

Rather than praise
and awe at your cool choice,
be braced for teasing, puzzlement
and weird questions from others.
You can also expect peer pressure,
trying to get you back into eating meat.

TURNING AND STAYING VEGGIE REQUIRES A BACKBONE ... YOURS!

A Veggie Life

RESEARCH AND ADVICE

Going veggie does require research, attention to detail and perseverance. Don't give up just because you've endured a couple of less-than-ideal meals in a row. Seek out others who are already vegetarian or are working towards that goal for support and practical advice. Swapping news, food and meal tips can make your whole veggie journey easier and more enjoyable.

SLIP-UPS

Some new or wannabe veggies find themselves slipping up occasionally. You might enjoy a meaty meal or find out something you thought was veggie actually contained animal products. Don't beat yourself up about it and instead of focusing on that food, think of all the meat-free meals you have already eaten and the positive contribution you have already made and will continue to make.

AND FINALLY ...

Turning completely vegetarian or vegan isn't for everyone at every point in their life. If you don't really like vegetables and pulses, be honest with yourself, or you'll make yourself ill! There's absolutely no shame in admitting to yourself that now isn't the right time after a period of trying it out. Who knows, you may turn veggie again in future months or years, or you may continue to enjoy some veggie meals but as a FLEXITARIAN (see page 11).

V-DAY

It's the big day, V-Day. You summon your family into the kitchen, living room or garden, clear your throat and drop the V bomb ... you're turning vegetarian. What happens next is partly up to you and your preparation.

BECOME VEGGIE EDUCATED

»»→ ADVICE IN ADVANCE ←«

Check out vegetarian cookbooks in libraries as well as the recipes in this book and on the Internet. It's well worth visiting your local **FOOD SHOPS** and seeing what's available. Staff at health food stores are often very knowledgeable and helpful. Make notes so you have ideas for your first veggie meals and any special ingredients they require.

PERFECT PLANNING

There's lots you can do before **V-DAY** to make things easier. Get your facts straight and your reasons for turning veggie clear in your head in advance. You might find it easier to arrange your thoughts on paper.

A Veggie Life

KEEP CALM AND VEGGIE ON

If family uproar occurs after your announcement, keep your cool. Stick to your messages and reasons but try to see things from your family's side. They might be worried about the cost, or worried you may not be getting enough protein and nutrients, or fearful that they will have to **GO VEGGIE, TOO**. Reassure them with what you have learned about healthy and affordable vegetarian meals and show them your notes or leaflets to emphasise the research you have done.

Reasons I want to go veggie...

1

2

KEEP CALM AND VEGGIE ON

⋅ HOME HELP ⋅

Point out any of your family meals that are already vegetarian or incredibly easy to turn vegetarian, such as sausages and mash with **VEGGIE SAUSAGES** and gravy for you. Try to be on your best behaviour throughout and offer to help with the shopping, cooking and extra washing-up your meals may create. You may only have to do this for a short time to get your family onside and used to you as a vegetarian.

YOUR SUBSTITUTES BENCH

There are hundreds of complete meal recipes available for veggies. But, sometimes, you may only be after a replacement for part of a meal such as the meat in a roast dinner, letting you enjoy the rest of the meal's vegetables and trimmings. Keep some of the items below in your family kitchen. Most can be cooked or heated easily and make great substitutes, such as a veggie burger in bread or hot falafel in pitta as a tasty alternative to a bacon or sausage sandwich.

FRIDGE-FREEZER

- VEGGIE BURGERS
- VEGGIE SAUSAGES
- VEGGIE MINCE
- FALAFELS
- A VEGGIE PIZZA
- VEGETABLE GRILLS OR PATTIES

CUPBOARD

- TINNED RATATOUILLE
- MIXED BEANS IN TOMATO OR (IF YOU PREFER) A SPICY SAUCE
- A DRIED NUT ROAST MIX
- TVP (TEXTURED VEGETABLE PROTEIN)
- JARS OF PASTA SAUCE
- TINNED VEGETARIAN SOUPS
- FLAVOURED PACKET RICE
- MIXED, UNSALTED NUTS

ONE-PAN IDEAS

It might seem like a silly complaint, but for the harassed household cook, a need to use a whole different set of pots and pans to feed the one veggie in a family can be a real headache. Try to help out, by picking simple, one-pan or one-oven tray alternatives for your part of a family meal. A veggie pasta meal, for instance, may only require one pan to gently cook some veggie mince, vegetables and sauce which can then be poured over your portion of pasta.

Celebrations

Certain mealtimes seem more important than others and as a new veggie, can appear daunting. Classic examples are Christmas dinner and celebratory meals like Thanksgiving or Easter. Some of these dinner dilemmas can be easily solved simply by replacing the slices of roast meat with a lovely hot quiche, nut roast or particularly tasty veggie pie. Avoid the meat gravy as well!

VEGGING OUT

A few weeks or months in to your veggie journey and you may be sitting smugly, having tamed your parents and even your older brother or sister into accepting you as a vegetarian. Brilliant! Well done! But there are further challenges ahead, away from home when eating out, at someone else's house or abroad on holiday.

SCHOOL LUNCH

It depends on your school district, but most school canteens offer vegetarian food although you may have to get your parents to specially request it. Taking packed lunches offers you lots more control over what you eat but pack-ups don't have to be just dull sandwiches. A veggie pasty or tart, grain salads such as bulgur or quinoa, rice crackers and dips, or a bean, cheese and salad-packed burrito or pitta pocket can give you a tasty energy punch at lunch.

OUT OF HOUSE

When invited round, it pays to check in advance. Don't assume the host knows you're veggie or even what that means. Many new veggies have been served tuna salad or fish fingers by a well-meaning host thinking that veggie means you simply don't eat red meat. Explain politely what you do and do not eat and, if it won't cause offence, make simple suggestions or offer to bring your own substitute for the meat part of the meal.

Meat-Free Menu

Many restaurants, cafés and diners have upped their veggie game in recent years. Most offer veggie options on their menus which are usually viewable on their website in advance. A phone call can also help if you have any specific questions such as whether a sauce is made with fish stock (an issue in some Thai and Chinese cooking).

Don't gamble on dinner out by not speaking up at the restaurant. Stay polite but firm when explaining your needs. Most eating places want you to enjoy your meal so you'll return and may make you a vegetarian dish that is not on the menu if you ask politely.

BBQ SEASON

Barbecue season used to be tough for veggies but not any more. There's lots of choice from pre-made veggie sausages and grills to vegetable skewers in sauce or barbecued aubergine stacked with a juicy portobello mushroom and topped with cheese for the ultimate veggie burger.

ON VEG-CATION!

Avoid holiday heartache in the same way as you would a disastrous dinner out by researching online. Check with your hotel or guesthouse or get your parents to send an email. All airlines offer at least one vegetarian meal, although these usually have to be booked at least 72 hours in advance.

TASTY TACOS IN MEXICO

DELICIOUS DESTINATIONS

Don't be put off by foreign country stereotypes. They're often wrong or don't tell the whole story. Germany, for example, is famous for its more than 1,500 different types of meaty sausage, but over seven million Germans — more than one in 12 of the entire population — are vegetarian, so there are plenty of options.

Once on holiday, keep a look out for suitable places to eat. Large resorts, towns and cities tend to feature a wide range of the world's cuisines and many of these offer plenty for veggies. These include: Mexican (vegetable and cheese burritos and fajitas), Italian (pizza, pasta and much more besides), Middle Eastern (falafels, couscous dishes, hummus), Indian and Nepalese (a vast range of vegetable curries and dishes) and South East Asian (satay tofu, coconut veggie curries, crispy stir-fries).

50

Camping brings its own special demands such as no freezer access and a reliance on one-pan meals. You might want to pack veggie burgers, sausages and other chiller foods in a cool box whilst tins of mixed beans, eggs (if you eat them) and mushrooms make quick and easy camp cookout options. Don't forget baked potatoes or whole sweetcorn wrapped in foil which can taste delicious after being cooked in a camp fire's embers.

SUN SCREEN

SPICY CURRY IN ASIA

ON THE CAMP FIRE

PASSPORT

GET COOKING

If you've decided to start living without meat, this section has some easy recipes to get you started. For more ideas, go to Jacqueline's blog: TINNEDTOMATOES.COM

BUT A FEW THINGS BEFORE YOU START ...

»»» YOUR INGREDIENTS «««

If you're going totally veggie, check that the ingredients you are using are suitable – for example buy vegetarian cheese. It's always best (and tastiest) to use free-range eggs as well. Peel onions and vegetables unless otherwise stated.

We've suggested you use vegetarian stock cubes for ease but home-made stock is quite easy to make. You can make a big batch and freeze it in ice-cube trays or little pots. There are recipes you can use online.

SWEET POTATO AND CARROT SOUP, PAGE 60

Make sure you have the ingredients you need for the recipe. It's really annoying if you're half way through and find out that you're missing a vital ingredient! Check that you have all of the equipment that you need too.

52

OVENS

Ovens should be preheated to the specified temperature. This usually takes around 15 minutes. Always ask an adult to help to turn the oven on for you and ask for help when using the hob. Use oven gloves when handling hot pans or baking trays. Remember to turn the hob and oven off when you have finished!

BROWNIES, PAGE 71

HEALTH AND SAFETY TIPS

1. WASH YOUR HANDS WITH SOAP AND WARM WATER BEFORE YOU START.
2. TIE BACK LONG HAIR.
3. RINSE AND DRY ALL FRUIT AND VEG THOROUGHLY.

ABBREVIATIONS

The following abbreviations have been used in the recipes:

tbsp tablespoon
tsp teaspoon
ml millilitre
g gram
kg kilogram

CLOUD EGGS

INGREDIENTS

- Eggs (one per person)
- Bread for toasting
- Butter

Breakfast eggs can be boiled, poached or scrambled, but they can be a bit boring. For a more EGGciting breakfast try these cloud eggs. The egg white is fluffy and light and the yolk is soft. Perfect on a slice of freshly buttered toast.

1. Preheat the oven to 230°C/210°C fan/450°F/Gas mark 8.

2. Carefully crack your egg. Pour the white into one bowl and the yolk into another.

3. Whisk the egg white into a firm meringue-like texture with a hand whisk or electric hand whisk. They should be quite firm and create peaks when you pull the whisk up through the mixture.

4. With a spoon, mound the egg white onto a baking tray and make a little dip in the centre for the egg yolk to sit in later, then pop the baking tray in the oven for 4-5 minutes until it's just beginning to turn golden.

5. Carefully take the baking tray out of the oven with an oven glove and place on top of the cooker. Gently pour the egg yolk into the dip in the middle of your meringue cloud and then pop it back into the oven for a couple of minutes.

6. Serve on buttered toast.

Tip: To separate the egg yolk and white, cup your hand over a bowl and have your assistant crack the egg into your hand (make sure your hands are lovely and clean first). Let the egg white slip through your fingers and then gently slide the egg yolk into another small bowl.

EGG-CEPTIONAL

CHOCOLATE CHIP AND RAISIN PANCAKES

INGREDIENTS

- 120 g self-raising four
- 30 g caster sugar
- A pinch of salt
- 50 g dark chocolate chips (optional)
- 50 g raisins (optional)
- 1 large egg
- ½ pint/1 cup/250 ml milk
- oil to grease the pan

MAKES 12 PANCAKES

At the weekend when you have more time it's nice to make something special for breakfast. These pancakes are simple to make and taste delicious. Serve them warm topped with butter, chocolate spread or a drizzle of maple syrup.

1. Sift the flour into a bowl, add the sugar, salt, chocolate chips and raisins (if using). Mix together with a spoon.

2. In a second bowl, whisk your milk and egg together. Make a well in the middle of your flour and pour in the egg mixture and whisk.

3. Use a piece of kitchen towel to rub your frying pan with a little oil and heat on a medium heat until the pan is hot.

4. When the pan is ready (see tip), pour in a tablespoon of batter. Each one will take about 3 minutes to cook. Turn each one over when they start to bubble. You can have a sneak peek underneath using a palette knife to check if they are ready to turn. They should be golden underneath.

5. Enjoy!

6. If you have too much batter, you can keep it in the fridge and use it the next day.

Tip: To find out if the pan is hot enough to make pancakes, pour a teaspoon of batter into the frying pan. The top should start to bubble in less than a minute. Flip it and cook the other side for just a few seconds. You should have a teeny golden pancake. If it doesn't bubble, let the pan heat a little longer.

YUM!

PINWHEEL SANDWICHES

INGREDIENTS

- 2 flour tortilla wraps
- 150 g mature cheddar, grated
- 5 tbsp sweetcorn
- 4 tbsp mayonnaise

SERVES 2

Pinwheel sandwiches are a fun alternative to regular sandwiches. Instead of bread they are made with soft flour tortilla wraps.

1. Grate the cheddar into a bowl and mix with the mayonnaise and sweetcorn.

2. Spread half of the filling over each tortilla. Don't take it right to the edge – leave a border with no filling.

3. Tuck the sides in and roll the tortillas into a sausage shape.

4. Chill in the fridge for 30 minutes. This makes them easier to cut.

5. Cut into pinwheel slices. Serve with some crunchy salad and a few crisps.

6. Enjoy!

MORE PINWHEEL SANDWICH FILLING IDEAS

Peanut butter and jam

Peanut butter and slices of banana

Cream cheese and cucumber

Cream cheese, slices of tomato and fresh basil

Cream cheese and strawberry jam

Cream cheese, thinly sliced apple and honey

Grated cheddar and pickle

Hummus, falafel (halved) and mango chutney

Hummus and grated carrot

Egg mayonnaise and cress

SWEET POTATO AND CARROT SOUP

INGREDIENTS

- 1 tbsp olive oil
- 1 onion, finely chopped
- 2 cloves of garlic, crushed
- 1 kg sweet potatoes, peeled and chopped
- 500 g carrots, grated
- 3 tsp ground cumin
- 2 tsp ground coriander
- 1 tsp chilli powder (optional)
- a handful of fresh coriander, chopped
- 1 ½ litres vegetable stock (hot)
- a pinch of salt and pepper

SERVES 6-8

A creamy soup with the sweetness of sweet potatoes and carrots, balanced with the warmth of spices. Easy to make, healthy and delicious. Have some bread or crackers ready for dunking!

1. In a large saucepan gently cook the onion and garlic in the olive oil until soft, stirring with a wooden spoon.

2. Add the carrots and sweet potatoes and cook gently for a few minutes before adding the cumin, ground coriander and chilli (if using).

3. Crumble three vegetable stock cubes into a litre measuring jug and carefully fill it with boiling water from the kettle. Stir carefully to dissolve and pour the liquid into the pan. Fill the jug up again, half way this time and pour that in too.

4. Increase the heat until the soup is bubbling, then turn it to low and cook for 30 minutes. Turn off the heat and add the fresh coriander.

5. Blend until smooth with a electric hand blender or with a potato masher. Ask for help with this as the soup will be very hot.

6. Season with a pinch of salt and pepper.

7. Leftovers can be kept in the fridge for two days or cooled and stored in tubs in the freezer.

SOUP-ER

61

10-MINUTE BEAN BURGERS

Homemade burgers are so much nicer than the ones you buy frozen and they are so much fun to make too. Your whole family will love these. Serve them in toasted burger buns with your favourite salad and toppings.

INGREDIENTS

- 800 g tinned kidney beans, rinsed well
- 400 g black beans, rinsed well
- 3 tsp ground cumin
- 2 tsp ground coriander
- 1 tsp chilli powder (more if you really want a kick)
- 90 g/1 cup porridge oats
- a generous handful of fresh coriander, chopped
- a good grinding of black pepper
- olive oil

MAKES 6-8 BURGERS

1. Rinse the beans in a colander and set aside a quarter of them in a bowl to add later, then pour the rest into a large bowl.

2. Mash the beans with a potato masher until you have a paste then add the herbs, spices, oats and whole beans to the bowl and mix with a spoon until well combined.

3. Shape the mixture into balls using your hands and then squash them into burger shapes.

4. These are now ready to cook. Heat a frying pan with a little olive oil and fry each side for a few minutes until crisp and starting to brown. You could also bake these on a baking tray in a hot oven for 20-25 minutes.

You can keep leftover burgers in the fridge for three days or freeze them on a tray, then when they are frozen pop them in a freezer bag. Burgers can be baked in the oven or fried in a little olive oil straight out of the freezer, but will take few minutes longer to cook on each side.

BEAN THERE, DONE THAT

A PIZZA CAKE

PUFF PIZZA PIES

INGREDIENTS

- 320 g ready-rolled puff pastry
- 4-5 tbsp tomato puree
- 125 g ball soft mozzarella, sliced thinly
- 8 cherry tomatoes or 4 salad tomatoes, sliced
- 1 tsp dried oregano

MAKES 8 PIZZAS (DEPENDING ON HOW BIG YOU MAKE THEM)

Making your own pizza is so satisfying, but kneading the dough and waiting for it to rise can take hours. I use ready-rolled puff pastry instead of pizza dough in this recipe.

1. Preheat the oven to 200°C/180°C fan/390°F/Gas mark 6.

2. Take the puff pastry out of the box and leave it on a plate to come to room temperature for 15 minutes before you make your pizzas.

3. Carefully unroll the pastry. Use a small bowl to cut circles out of the pastry. Press down and give it a wiggle. You may need to use a knife, but the bowl should cut through the pastry. Place the circles onto two floured baking trays, leaving a good space between each one.

4. Top each pastry circle with a dollop of tomato puree. Spread it carefully with the back of a teaspoon, leaving a small border around the edge.

5. Top with a slice of mozzarella and slices of tomato.

6. Sprinkle each pizza with a little oregano.

7. Bake the pizzas for 15 minutes until the pastry is golden and the cheese has melted. Serve with some salad.

QUICK GREEN SPAGHETTI SAUCE

A vibrant green sauce for pasta that's made in minutes. It's packed with goodness, super creamy and it coats the pasta beautifully.

INGREDIENTS

- 300 g spaghetti
- 1 ripe avocado, skin and stone removed
- 100 g frozen peas
- 1 handful spinach leaves
- 1 handful fresh coriander
- 1 handful fresh parsley
- 4 tbsp vegetarian parmesan* or mature cheddar
- 200 ml milk
- A pinch of salt and pepper

* Sometimes called 'hard cheese'

SERVES 4

1. Cook the spaghetti in a large pan of boiling water according to the packet instructions, then drain and return to the pot.

2. While the spaghetti is cooking, whizz up the avocado, peas, spinach, herbs, cheese and milk in a blender or food processor.

3. Season with a pinch of salt and pepper.

4. Pour the sauce over your cooked spaghetti, stir in and warm a little over a low heat.

5. Serve in bowls topped with a sprinkle of cheese.

6. Enjoy!

PASTA THE BOWL, PLEASE

SPINACH AND COCONUT DAL

A delicious family meal that can be thrown together in under half an hour, and it tastes delicious. Serve the dal with rice, poppadoms and mango chutney or just with some toasted pitta bread for dunking.

INGREDIENTS

- 400 g red lentils
- 400 ml tin of coconut milk
- 600 ml hot vegetable stock
- 2 tsp ground cumin
- 1 tsp ground coriander
- 1 tsp ground ginger
- 1 tsp turmeric
- 1 tsp chilli powder (optional)
- 200 g spinach
- a good grinding of black pepper

SERVES 4-6

1. Rinse the lentils well in a fine sieve under cold running water then pour them into a large pot with all the ingredients except for the spinach and black pepper.

2. Bring the dal to the boil over a medium heat, then reduce the heat until you have a gentle simmer and cook for 15 minutes, stirring occasionally.

3. Add the spinach and cook for another 5-10 minutes or until the lentils are soft.

4. You may need to add a little more stock or water, if you think it is too thick.

5. Season with black pepper and serve.

RICE TO MEET YOU

EASY CHOCOLATE MOUSSE

SPEEDY

INGREDIENTS

- 249 g silken tofu
- 3 ripe bananas
- 3 heaped tbsp cocoa powder
- a generous squirt of squeezy honey (optional)
- whipped cream and sprinkles (optional)

SERVES 4

An indulgent chocolate mousse that's made in minutes and is divinely chocolatey. It's the perfect last minute dessert.

1. Drain the tofu and pop into a blender.

2. Peel the bananas and pop them into the blender too with the cocoa powder and honey.

3. Whizz until smooth.

4. Pour into four small glasses or dessert jars and chill until needed.

5. Top with whipped cream and sprinkles if you like.

CHOCOLATE BROWNIES

INGREDIENTS

- 200 g dark chocolate, broken into pieces
- 200 g butter
- 3 large eggs
- 1 tsp vanilla extract
- 200 g light brown sugar
- 80 g plain flour, sieved
- a pinch of salt

MAKES 16 BROWNIES

Why not top these lovely brownies with your favourite chocolate sweets?

1. Preheat the oven to 180°C/160°C fan/350°F/ Gas mark 4.

2. Melt the chocolate and butter in a bain marie (a bowl over gently simmering water, making sure the bowl doesn't touch the water or the chocolate could be ruined).

3. Whisk the eggs with the sugar and vanilla extract until light and frothy, then pour into the chocolate mixture and mix in.

4. Line a baking tin (25 x 20 x 3.5 cm) with baking parchment. Fold in the flour and salt and pour the brownie batter into the tin. Bake for 20-25 minutes.

5. Leave to cool then pop in the fridge overnight.

6. For extra luxury, top with chocolate buttercream and sprinkles. Enjoy!

STRAWBERRY CHEESECAKE NO-CHURN ICE CREAM

INGREDIENTS

- 400 g strawberries
- 4 tbsp caster sugar
- 1 tbsp lemon juice
- 397 g condensed milk
- 280 g cream cheese
- 1 tsp vanilla extract
- 600 ml double cream
- 4 digestive biscuits

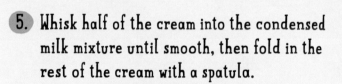

MAKES 1 LARGE
TUB OF ICE CREAM

This is a gloriously creamy dessert that you can make at home and you don't need an ice cream maker.

1. Chop the strawberries into quarters, leaving a few whole for decoration. Add the chopped strawberries to a pan with the lemon juice and caster sugar. Bring to a boil over a medium heat, then turn the heat down to low and let the mixture bubble away for 5-10 minutes until it has thickened. Leave to cool. The mixture is very hot so don't touch it.

2. Place the biscuits in a bag and crush them with a rolling pin.

3. In a large bowl whisk the condensed milk, cream cheese and vanilla extract together until smooth. You can use a hand whisk or an electric hand mixer for this.

4. Clean the blades of the whisk or mixer. Then, in another large bowl, whisk up the double cream until it forms soft peaks.

5. Whisk half of the cream into the condensed milk mixture until smooth, then fold in the rest of the cream with a spatula.

6. Pour a third of the ice cream into a tub or baking tin, then drizzle with some of the strawberry sauce and sprinkle over some of the biscuit crumbs. Repeat for another two layers.

7. Slice the remaining strawberries and use them to decorate the top of the ice cream, then pop the tub or tin in the freezer and leave to set overnight.

8. Take the ice cream out of the freezer 30 minutes before you want to serve it.

COCONUT ICE

INGREDIENTS

- 2 bowls, each filled with 125 g of icing sugar
- 2 bowls, each filled with 100 g of condensed milk
- 2 bowls, each filled with 100 g of desiccated coconut
- a few drops of pink food colouring

Coconut ice is an old-fashioned sweet treat you can make at home. You will need a 20 cm square baking tin and a few bowls to prepare the ingredients in.

1. Line your tin with tinfoil or greaseproof paper. Make sure it shows above the top of the tin to make it easier to lift out.

2. Add 100 g of desiccated coconut to a sealable bag (freezer bags are good for this), then add a few drops of pink food colouring. Make sure the bag is sealed properly then shake until the coconut turns pink. Set aside until you are ready to make your pink layer.

3. Sift 125 g icing sugar into a large bowl, then add 100 g of white desiccated coconut and 100 g of condensed milk.

4. Stir well, then bring together the white mixture into a ball with your hands.

5. Press the white coconut ice into your tin. You want it to be between 1 and 1.5 cm deep. Smooth the top of the coconut ice with the back of a spoon until it is smooth and even.

6. Start your pink layer next. Sift 125 g icing sugar into a bowl, add 100 g of pink coconut and 100 g of condensed milk. Mix well, pull together in to ball and press into the tin on top of the white layer. Smooth this layer with a spoon.

7. Lift the coconut ice carefully out of the tin by firmly holding the edges of the foil or paper and move it to a baking rack to dry out for three hours. After three hours, cut into squares. Store in an airtight container, so it doesn't dry out any more.

SWEET!

VEG ON THE WEB

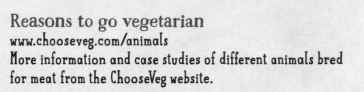

Reasons to go vegetarian

www.chooseveg.com/animals
More information and case studies of different animals bred for meat from the ChooseVeg website.

https://vegsoc.org/wp-content/uploads/2019/02/Why-Its-Green.pdf
A downloadable 20-page booklet, *Why it's green to go vegetarian*

www.peta.org/issues/animals-used-for-food/meat-environment
An informative article summarising some of the impacts on the planet of the meat and fishing industries, produced by PETA (People for the Ethical Treatment of Animals).

Cruelty to animals

www.ciwf.org.uk/get-involved
Explore the Compassion in World Farming website to find out about the work of this animal welfare charity. It includes advice on how to improve the lives of farm animals by changing your family's food shopping habits.

www.rspcaassured.org.uk/farm-animal-welfare
Find out about the RSPCA's farm animal welfare standards.

http://features.peta.org/cruelty-free-company-search/index.aspx
Search for cruelty-free cosmetics, personal care products and more using the PETA searchable database.

www.crueltyfreeinternational.org/LeapingBunny
Search for Leaping Bunny certified cruelty-free products using this weblink.

www.vegsoc.org/veggieaware
The Vegetarian Society's 'Veggie aware A-Z' will help you avoid products that may have involved cruelty to animals.

Healthy living

www.choosemyplate.gov/ten-tips-healthy-eating-for-vegetarians
The home of the US government's MyPlate initiative for healthy eating has quizzes, tools and advice pages such as these tips for vegetarian eating.

https://vegsoc.org/product/veggie-guide-for-teens-and-parents/
A useful downloadable guide for teens and their parents from the Vegetarian Society.

www.nhs.uk/Livewell/Goodfood/Pages/the-eatwell-guide.aspx
This Eatwell guide is presented by the UK's National Health Service (NHS).

www.viva.org.uk/resources/campaign-materials/guide/healthy-veggie-kids
A downloadable Healthy Veggie Kids booklet by Viva! charity founder, Juliet Gellatley.

www.vegansociety.com/go-vegan
The Vegan Society has a website packed with information and recipes.

Quick recipes
One-pan meals and veggie breakfasts are a blast with these recipe websites.

https://vegsoc.org/recipes/?_difficulty=simple
Downloadable information leaflets and recipe ideas from the Vegetarian Society.

www.marthastewart.com/1119146/one-pot-vegetarian-meals
A scrummy collection of one-pot veggie meals by Martha Stewart.

www.bbcgoodfood.com/recipes/collection/vegetarian-breakfast
Wake up to wonderful breakfast times with 30 delicious recipes from BBC Good Food.

www.jamieoliver.com/news-and-features/features/ultimate-veggie-bbq/
Some delicious and simple veggie BBQ recipes from British chef, Jamie Oliver.

www.onegreenplanet.org/vegan-food/epic-veggie-burgers-to-throw-on-the-grill-now/
Ten stunning veggie burgers that will even make meat-eaters' mouths water.

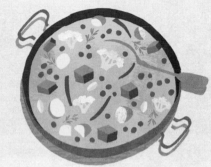

Eating out
Here are some useful websites for researching eating out, veggie-style.

www.vegguide.org
A handy database of vegetarian and vegan-friendly restaurants, cafés and shops, searchable by continent, country and city.

www.happycow.net
Another database of restaurants and shops all over the world plus a great travel article section with lots of top tips.

www.vegdining.com/Home.cfm
A useful, searchable directory of places to eat which are either purely vegetarian or veggie friendly.

Special occasion cooking
Check out some great ideas for special occasions vegetarian cooking:

www.stylist.co.uk/life/recipes/25-alternatives-to-nut-roast-2-vegetarian-food
A sensational selection of 25 special veggie recipes – from parmesan snowflakes to mushroom wellington.

GLOSSARY

antibiotics A substance used to kill bacteria and treat infections.

atmosphere The blanket of gases that surround a planet.

bland Dull and lacking flavour (when used to describe food).

blog A journal or diary published online and made available to others via the Internet.

calcium A mineral which is essential for healthy bones and teeth.

carbohydrates Substances, such as sugars and starches, found in many foods including bread, pasta, potatoes and rice, which help provide the body with energy.

carnivore A creature that lives completely or almost completely through eating other creatures.

deforestation The cutting down or burning of forests for wood or to create space for farmland or settlements.

E-numbers Code numbers for substances added to food which are listed amongst the food's ingredients.

factory-farmed A system of intensive farming where lots of animals are kept in a small, closed area, to produce as much food as cheaply as possible.

fibre (dietary) A substance found in wholegrain cereals and fruit and vegetables which is essential for a healthy diet.

flexitarian A person who mostly eats a vegetarian diet but sometimes eats meat or fish.

greenhouse gases Gases in the atmosphere which help trap and hold heat and contribute to the greenhouse effect, such as carbon dioxide (CO_2), nitrous oxide and methane.

habitat The home or natural environment in which a plant or creature usually lives.

herbivore A creature that survives solely by eating plants.

humane To show care and kindness, and to reduce suffering as much as possible.

minerals Substances, such as calcium and potassium, found in food that your body needs for growth and health.

nutrients Any substance that plants or animals need in order to live and grow.

nutrition The study of food and how it works in your body.

omnivore A creature which can eat plants and meat in its usual diet.

peer pressure Strong influence of a group on its members to behave as the rest of the group does.

protein Substances which build, maintain and replace tissues in your body. Protein is found in a wide variety of foods including meat, fish, nuts, eggs, beans and dairy products.

quinoa A slightly crunchy small grain which is gluten-free and can be used in salads, soups and other dishes.

rennet A substance that comes from the stomach of newly-born calves.

respiration A chemical process in which energy is released from food substances, such as sugars.

saturated fats A type of fat found in, for example, processed and fatty meats, hard cheeses, whole milk and cream, butter, lard, palm oil and coconut oil.

soil erosion The wearing away and disappearance of the most fertile layer of soil, the topsoil, leading to a loss of plant life and homes for creatures.

stereotype A fixed and often unfair or incorrect idea about a group of people who share one characteristic, that they are all the same.

suffocate To die due to lack of air or being unable to breathe.

iNDEX

Taoist Someone who follows the Chinese philosophy of Taoism.

tofu Also known as soyabean curd, this food is made by forming soya milk into solid curds in a similar way to how cheese is made from milk.

UNICEF Part of the United Nations which focuses on giving aid and support to children around the world.

vitamins A group of substances that the human body needs in small quantities to function well. They are usually not made within the body but are found within foods.